DATE DUE

DEMCO 128-5046

BASKETBALL LEGENDS

Kareem Abdul-Jabbar

Charles Barkley

Larry Bird

Wilt Chamberlain

Clyde Drexler

Julius Erving

Patrick Ewing

Anfernee Hardaway

Grant Hill

Magic Johnson

Michael Jordan

Jason Kidd

Reggie Miller

Hakeem Olajuwon

Shaquille O'Neal

Scottie Pippen

David Robinson

Dennis Rodman

CHELSEA HOUSE PUBLISHERS

BASKETBALL LEGENDS

HAKEEM OLAJUWON

Fred McMane

Introduction by
Chuck Daly

CHELSEA HOUSE PUBLISHERS
Philadelphia

Produced by Daniel Bial and Associates
New York, New York

Picture research by Alan Gottlieb
Cover illustration by Bradford Brown

First Printing

1 3 5 7 9 8 6 4 2

Library of Congress Cataloging-in-Publication Data

McMane, Fred.
    Hakeem Olajuwon / Fred McMane; introduction by Chuck Daly.
    p. cm. — (Basketball legends)
    Includes bibliographical references and index.
ISBN 0-7910-4385-1 (hardcover)
1. Olajuwon, Hakeem, 1963–   —Juvenile literature. 2. Basketball players—United
States—Biography—Juvenile literature. 3. Houston Rockets (Basketball team)—
Juvenile literature. I. Title. II. Series.
GV884.O43M39   1997
796.323'092—dc20
[B]   96-34779
                                                                        CIP
                                                                         AC

CONTENTS

BECOMING A
BASKETBALL LEGEND

Chuck Daly

What does it take to be a basketball superstar? Two of the three things it takes are easy to spot. Any great athlete must have excellent skills and tremendous dedication. The third quality needed is much harder to define, or even put in words. Others call it leadership or desire to win, but I'm not sure that explains it fully. This third quality relates to the athlete's thinking process, a certain mentality and work ethic. One can coach athletic skills, and while few superstars need outside influence to help keep them dedicated, it is possible for a coach to offer some well-timed words in order to keep that athlete fully motivated. But a coach can do no more than appeal to a player's will to win; how much that player is then capable of ensuring victory is up to his own internal workings.

In recent times, we have been fortunate to have seen some of the best to play the game. Larry Bird, Magic Johnson, and Michael Jordan had all three components of superstardom in full measure. They brought their teams to numerous championships, and made the players around them better. (They also made their coaches look smart.)

I myself coached a player who belongs in that class, Isiah Thomas, who helped lead the Detroit Pistons to consecutive NBA crowns. Isiah is not tall-he's just over six feet-but he could do whatever he wanted with the ball. And what he wanted to do most was lead and win.

All the players I mentioned above and those whom this series will chronicle are tremendously gifted athletes, but for the most part, you can't play professional basketball at all unless you have excellent skills. And few players get to stay on their team unless they are willing to dedicate themselves to improving their talents even more, learning about their opponents, and finding a way to join with their teammates and win.

It's that third element that separates the good player from the superstar, the memorable players from the legends of the game. Superstars know when to take over the game. If the situation calls for a defensive stop, the superstars stand up and do it. If the situation calls for a key pass, they make it. And if the situation calls for a big shot, they want the ball. They don't want the ball simply because of their own glory or ego. Instead they know—and their teammates know—that they are the ones who can deliver, regardless of the pressure.

The words "legend" and "superstar" are often tossed around without real meaning. Taking a hard look at some of those who truly can be classified as "legends" can provide insight into the things that brought them to that level. All of them developed their legacy over numerous seasons of play, even if certain games will always stand out in the memories of those who saw them. Those games typically featured amazing feats of all-around play. No matter how great the fans thought the superstars were, these players were capable of surprising the fans, their opponents, and occasionally even themselves. The desire to win took over, and with their dedication and athletic skills already in place, they were capable of the most astonishing achievements.

CHUCK DALY, most recently the head coach of the New Jersey Nets, guided the Detroit Pistons to two straight NBA championships, in 1989 and 1990. He earned a gold medal as coach of the 1992 U.S. Olympic basketball team—the so-called "Dream Team"—and was inducted into the Pro Basketball Hall of Fame in 1994.

1

THE PROUD WARRIOR

It is the biggest game of Hakeem Olajuwon's basketball career, and his parents aren't there. Ever since he first picked up a basketball at the age of 17 in his birthplace of Lagos, Nigeria, and allowed the game to dominate his life, he had waited for this moment. He had wanted to share it with his parents, but they can't bring themselves to watch.

Salaam and Abike Olajuwon had intended to be sitting at courtside ever since Game 1 of the 1994 National Basketball Association (NBA) championship series with the New York Knicks, but they cannot bear it. The game is too violent for them. There is too much physical contact. They are content to watch on television, but even then they don't stay tuned for too long. Just a quick glance to check the score.

It is too bad because they will be missing one of the classic face-to-face showdowns in NBA

Hakeem Olajuwon works with the ball in the low post against Patrick Ewing of the Knicks during the 1994 NBA finals.

history between two of the league's most gallant warriors. On this day the 6'10" Hakeem will once again wage a hard battle against a respected foe, 7'0" Patrick Ewing of the Knicks.

Ewing has been lurking in the back of Olajuwon's mind for quite some time. It has been 10 years since they met face-to-face in a championship game. Both of them were in college then, Hakeem at the University of Houston and Ewing at Georgetown University. Georgetown beat Houston that day for the NCAA title. Ewing went on to be selected by the Knicks as the number one pick in the 1985 NBA draft but had yet to lead his team to a championship.

Hakeem became a number one pick in 1984 and had spent the next decade trying to prove that the Houston Rockets were justified in taking him over Michael Jordan and Charles Barkley. While Jordan had led the Chicago Bulls to three NBA championships by 1994, Hakeem, like Ewing, was in search of his first. Until that happened, neither player could stand next to the great centers of the game like Bill Russell, Wilt Chamberlain, or Kareem Abdul-Jabbar, each of whom owned more than one championship ring.

During the Western Conference finals with Utah, Olajuwon admitted he often found himself thinking about Ewing instead of the man he was guarding at the time, Felton Spencer of the Jazz. Ewing would be on Olajuwon's mind during practice sessions and even on off days.

"Way back, maybe five or eight years ago, I would look at the championship series and I would think to myself: 'Wow, what if I meet somebody like Patrick in the championship?'" Olajuwon said. "I looked at [Michael] Jordan and Magic [Johnson], and Jordan and Clyde Drexler — a dream matchup. I tried to imagine it, but it seemed like such a long shot: if I got there maybe Patrick wouldn't get there, or if he got there maybe I wouldn't.

"This year when I looked at the playoffs it became more and more realistic. It was always in the back of my mind. I didn't want to over-look the team that we are playing, but every once in a while it crossed my mind — playing that championship game — Patrick and I. I have all these flashbacks when I played against him all these years trying to think 'What did I do best against him?' Thinking about the moves that I used that were most effective so I can start preparing."

Hakeem holds nothing but the utmost respect for the Knicks' center. "With Patrick it's all men-tal because I respect his ability so much," said Olajuwon. "That's what makes me prepare for him and try to play smarter and try to exploit different areas, his weaknesses. Most of the big men today keep their hands down; when he's in the middle I feel his presence. Patrick is a true example of a big man. He's the classic example. And he's a winner."

So far in this series, though, Hakeem has proven to be the more versatile player. Voted the league Most Valuable Player during the regular season, Hakeem has demonstrated his all-round skills repeatedly as the two teams battled to a 3-3 standoff over the first six games.

Although he is dog-tired from all the pounding he has received, Hakeem has outplayed Ewing in the first six games of the series, but the Rock-ets have not been able to shake off the Knicks.

They cannot break loose from New York on this night either. With Hakeem showing off his unstoppable turn-around jumper and creating havoc on defense for Ewing underneath the basket, Houston scratches to a 45-43 lead at the half.

The two-point deficit, though, is misleading. All season long the Knicks had relied heavily on the scoring of Ewing and guard John Starks and neither is having a very good game. Starks is being hounded by Houston's Vernon Maxwell and cannot find the basket. Ewing's shot is not dropping either.

Led by Hakeem and Maxwell, the Rockets streak to an eight-point lead with 1:48 left in the third quarter. The Knicks fight back, drawing to within three points with 2:51 remaining in the game. But then Hakeem takes over. With the Knicks putting the pressure on, Olajuwon not once — but twice — lifts his team.

Charles Oakley makes two free throws to pull New York to within 78-75, but Olajuwon answers with a tough hook shot over Ewing to boost the margin to five points.

Olajuwon smiles as NBA commissioner David Stern is about to present the championship trophy. Announcer Bob Costas is at right.

The Knicks zip the ball upcourt to Ewing who tries a nine-foot jumper from the left baseline with Olajuwon bothering his shot. The Rockets get the rebound and work it into Olajuwon at the other end of the court. The Knicks quickly double-team him and he passes the ball out to Maxwell, who calmly hits a three-point shot from 25 feet out to give Houston a commanding eight-point advantage. The Knicks never get closer than four points and the Rockets win, 90-84, to bring the city of Houston its first championship in any sport.

Hakeem finishes with 25 points, 10 rebounds, and 7 assists and clearly outplays Ewing, who struggles through a miserable 7 of 17 shooting performance and manages just 17 points while turning the ball over five times.

Starks, too, suffers through an excruciating, painful shooting performance. He misses all 11 of his three-point attempts and scores just 8 points. Meanwhile, Maxwell gets 21 in his best game of the series, and Rockets' rookie guard Sam Cassell chips in with 13.

As the two big men leave the court after the game, Hakeem catches up to Ewing and put his arm around him. "I didn't get a chance to see him to talk to him on the floor but on the way out I had an opportunity to talk," he said. "We gave each other a hug. I told him, hopefully maybe next year. He deserves it."

To no one's surprise, Hakeem is named the Most Valuable Player of the series. He averaged 26.9 points, 9.1 rebounds, and 3.9 blocked shots for the seven games.

"This championship game will kick him over the top, as it should," said Knicks' coach Pat Riley.

2
"COCOA ONE"

One could say that Hakeem Abdul Olajuwon had been on top since his birth. The name Olajuwon means "always being on top" and Hakeem is Arabic for "wise one."

Hakeem was born in Lagos, Nigeria, on January 21, 1963. Nigeria, located on the western part of Africa, is a bit larger than the states of Texas and Oklahoma combined. It has the largest population of all the African nations — more than 88 million people, or about one-third the population of the United States. Lagos was the capital of Nigeria while Hakeem was growing up and remains its largest city with a population of 1.4 million people.

Hakeem was the third child born in a middle class family of five boys and one girl. He has an older brother, Kaka; an older sister, Kudi; and three younger brothers: Akins, Taju and Afis.

In the early 1960s, Sherman Rosenberg of Chicago introduced basketball to Nigeria while teaching chemistry at Queens College in Lagos.

15

Although many people in Nigeria are poor, Hakeem had a comfortable life. His father, Salaam, was in the cement business, serving as a broker between wholesalers and retailers. "In Nigeria sports is more like a hobby," said Hakeem. "There is no future for sports as a profession. So, my father did not discourage sports, but he did not encourage it either. He encouraged education more than anything else."

Hakeem's parents expected each child to go to another country to attend college. Kaka, the oldest, studied in London, England, while Kudi was schooled at the American University in Cairo, Egypt. Both then returned home to live.

Basketball would steer a different course for Hakeem and two of his younger brothers. All three would earn basketball scholarships to U.S. colleges, Hakeem to the University of Houston and Taju and Afis to the University of Texas at San Antonio. All three eventually made lives for themselves in Houston where they were joined by Akins.

Hakeem found out early in his life that he was better than most of the other children in sports. He excelled at soccer, where he played defense and goalie, and at team handball, a sport that has some similarities to basketball and is very popular in countries outside the United States.

Hakeem also found out very early in life that he was going to be much taller than his friends. By the time he was 15 he had already grown to 6'9". That made him the subject of ridicule from some of his classmates. They would taunt him about his size and often he would get into fights.

"Sometimes I would be ashamed of being tall," said Olajuwon. "I would wish I was a normal height so I can be friendly like everybody else.

Everywhere I went, people were looking. My parents knew why I was always fighting and they tried to encourage me about my height."

At the age of 12, Hakeem entered a boarding school. There he came in contact with youngsters from different Nigerian tribes. Two-thirds of the population of Nigeria are members of the Hausa, Yoruba, Ibo, or Fulani tribes. Hakeem was a member of the Yoruban tribe. Since each tribe spoke its own regional language, Nigerians were taught English to communicate with one another. Hakeem learned to respect and appreciate the differences among people.

Hakeem attended a school, called Moslem Teachers College, until he graduated at the age of 17. He starred in soccer, team handball, and field hockey for his school team. He also was an excellent high jumper.

One day while he was playing soccer he was approached by Oscar Johnson, coach of the Nigerian national basketball team. Although he was 6'9", Hakeem had never played basketball before. He had been asked many times but had always politely refused to give it a try.

"The handball court was about two minutes from the basketball court and all these coaches had been trying to get me to a basketball court, but I didn't show any interest," Olajuwon recalled. "They cannot get me there because I love handball. I was closed minded. I did not even want to look at basketball because I enjoyed my sports."

Johnson, however, was more persuasive than the others. He convinced Hakeem to come to the

Two of Hakeem Olajuwon's brothers, Taju (top) and Afis, also came to study in the United States.

basketball court with him. While the two were talking, Johnson began shooting at the basket. Then he passed the ball to Hakeem and asked him to shoot. Hakeem's first shot missed everything, an air ball.

Hakeem was embarrassed but the competitive juices stirred within him. He did not want Johnson to think he was uncoordinated so he asked to try another shot. He shot another air ball, then another. Johnson showed Hakeem some of the finer techniques in shooting and finally Hakeem made a basket. After that he didn't want to stop. The two men stayed on the court shooting for two hours.

Hakeem was now hooked on the sport. He soon dropped his other sports and concentrated solely on basketball. He was only 16 but was placed on the national basketball team so that he could learn the rules of the game.

"I was his [Johnson's] special project," said Hakeem. "I was abnormal because I was taller than all of the kids, because Nigerians on the average are short. So I always stood out in the crowd and I was criticized and people made fun of me. I wasn't comfortable. I felt I was too tall.

"My father was concerned because most of the tall guys ended up bent over because they didn't want to stand straight. They tried to hide. They were not proud that they are tall. That's the one thing my family made me understand — stand tall, be proud. I started believing it."

Hakeem developed a reputation as a premier shot-blocker. He joined a Nigerian club team sponsored by a European company, Leventis. Soon he had a small legion of fans. After each basket that the team scored, the players would raise their index finger in the air and shout,

"Cocoa One." Hakeem scored so many baskets that "Cocoa One" became his nickname.

Hakeem had hoped someday to get an opportunity to further his education in the United States. It was becoming apparent that basketball would pave the road for him to fulfill that ambition.

3

THE DREAM

Every boy dreams. But in Nigeria, the dreams are not of untold riches made playing professional sports in the United States. Those kind of dreams are not realistic in places such as Lagos. A realistic one is about going to the United States in order to get an education. This was a dream that Hakeem had harbored since his early days at school.

In the summer of 1980, that dream began to become a reality. Hakeem was playing in the African Junior Championships in Angola and when the tournament ended he was approached by an American, Christopher Pond, a U.S. State Department employee who had coached Hakeem's team in the tournament.

Pond gave Hakeem a list of college coaches who might be able to offer him a basketball scholarship. Pond also gave Hakeem the name of a person to contact to make the arrangements for travel to the United States.

Hakeem Olajuwon outbattles Cozell McQueen of North Carolina State University in the NCAA championship game in 1983.

"The day I arrived in New York, it was cold, so I went to Houston where I was told it was warm," said Hakeem. "When nobody met me at the airport, I called and the coach told me to take a cab to the school."

Guy Lewis, a veteran coach who had produced several All-Americans at the University of Houston, including Elvin Hayes, had been tipped about Hakeem from a friend who was coaching the Central African junior national team. Based on his experience, Lewis expected Hakeem to be shorter and less skilled than his friend had indicated.

Coach Lewis was pleasantly surprised to find that Hakeem was truly 6' 9", but when he saw him play for the first time he knew he did not yet have the skills to play on a collegiate level.

So shy was the Nigerian youngster that he didn't even bother to correct anyone when his first name was misspelled as "Akeem" during enrollment at the university. It would be 11 years before he would announce to the world that he preferred the correct Arabic spelling of his name.

Hakeem was a friendly person but kept to himself in his first year at the University of Houston because he needed time to adjust to new surroundings. He needed to get used to college, to American food and American customs. Hakeem spoke English with a British accent and sometimes his teammates would laugh at him because he sounded so formal when he talked. He spoke English, French, and four African dialects but he knew nothing of American ways. But the rest of the team made Hakeem feel comfortable.

Hakeem was polite to everyone. At first, he even bowed when he greeted his teammates. But that made them laugh, too, and he quickly stopped that custom.

Hakeem was very skinny — weighing only 190 pounds — when he arrived at Houston and coach Lewis wanted him to put on weight. But Hakeem missed his favorite foods from Nigeria, like fried bananas, hot, spicy rice, and fufu, a stew poured over baked dough.

At first, Hakeem was homesick for Nigeria. He called his family at least twice a week. But his teammates did their best to make him feel more comfortable.

"Campus life was a wonderful life for me," Hakeem said. "It didn't take long for me to adjust because I was on campus and I was just so excited to be a student at the University of Houston, going to class every morning."

The thing he liked best about the United States was that for the first time in his life he could get shoes that fit. Back home in Nigeria the biggest shoes he could find were a size 14. They were too small and it would take months before he could stretch those shoes enough to make them feel comfortable on his feet. In the United States he found shoes in size 16. "They felt like I had no shoes on at all," he said.

Another thing he liked was that in America, no one thought there was anything wrong with being tall. In fact, it was good to be tall, especially if you wanted to play college basketball.

Clyde Drexler and Hakeem Olajuwon show off some of the souvenir merchandise celebrating their high-flying team.

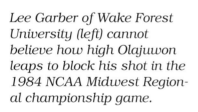

Lee Garber of Wake Forest University (left) cannot believe how high Olajuwon leaps to block his shot in the 1984 NCAA Midwest Regional championship game.

Hakeem, though, did not get to play on the team his first year at Houston. Coach Lewis did not think Hakeem knew enough about basketball or was strong enough to play against the kind of competition that Houston faced. So Hakeem was "redshirted," meaning he could practice with the team but could not play in games. All athletes are eligible to play college sports over a five-year period. But they may compete in only four of those years. The year they don't play is called a "redshirt" year. The term was derived from these ineligible players being assigned red shirts during practice sessions.

Although Hakeem could not play, he was made to feel part of the team by the other members of the squad. Coach Lewis sent him to the weight room every day to bulk up his thin frame. Coach Lewis also taught him how to use his size to advantage underneath the basket and how to utilize his jumping ability and quickness.

"He didn't know how to post up. He had no power move to the basket, he had no turnaround shot," Coach Lewis recalled. "He could jump, but he didn't know when to jump or where to jump."

Still, he excited people with his raw ability. Playing for fun in a pick-up game one day at the university during the summer of his freshman year, Hakeem heard people shouting his name from the stands. "Hakeem the Dream," came the cries. He had not started a varsity game but already he had a new nickname.

One of the players appearing in the summer pickup games was Moses Malone, the star center for the Houston Rockets. He took a liking to Hakeem and became sort of a big brother. He helped Hakeem improve his game. "He'd push me around most of the time," Hakeem recalled. "Anytime I went up for a dunk on him, he'd push me so I couldn't make the dunk."

As a sophomore, Hakeem had progressed far enough to make the team as a backup center to starter Larry Micheaux. Hakeem wanted to start, but Coach Lewis said he was not ready. Whenever he did play he got himself in foul trouble.

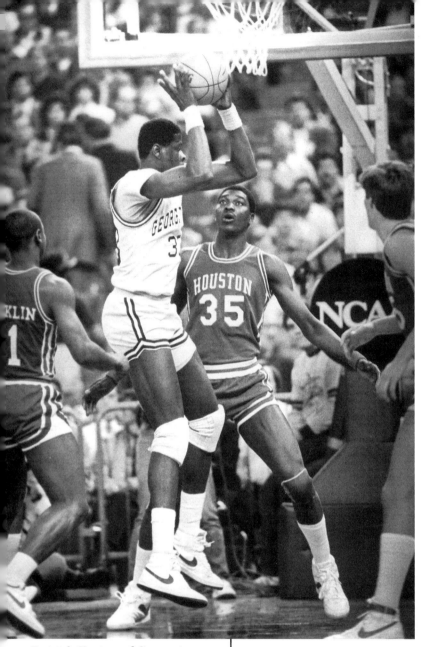

Patrick Ewing of Georgetown University corrals a rebound in the 1984 championship game. Olajuwon and Ewing would play big games against one another in the pros.

As a result he played only about 18 minutes a game.

"He would play five minutes and be exhausted," said Coach Lewis. "He'd play 10 and foul out. I kept him out of games. I wouldn't let him practice until he could run. That first year he never did get to where he could play a full game. He actually hurt us in there."

Still, the team did well, finishing 21-7 in the Southwest Conference. The Cougars finished in second place in both the regular season and Southwest Conference tournament. That enabled the Cougars to get invited to participate in the National College Athletic Conference (NCAA) tournament.

The tournament was the nation's first look at Hakeem. He played well in the first three rounds as Houston advanced to the Midwest division finals. The Cougars met Boston College, but Hakeem got into early foul trouble and was of little help. Houston managed to win the game anyway and advanced to the Final Four, or semifinals of the tournament. There they came up against the University of North Carolina, which had a freshman player named Michael Jordan.

Coach Lewis did not start Hakeem in the game and North Carolina built an early 10-point lead. Hakeem played only 20 minutes against North Carolina. He scored two points and grabbed six rebounds but the Tar Heels won, 64-63.

Hakeem worked again that summer with Malone and by the start of the 1982-83 season he was ready to start. Coach Lewis moved Micheaux to forward and the Cougars became the strongest team in college basketball. Hakeem started at center for a run-and-gun team that won 25 straight games and spent most of the 1982-83 season ranked number one in the nation. The team was exciting and played an above-the-rim type of game that electrified the crowd.

The star of the team was Clyde "The Glide" Drexler, a 6'-6" forward who would swoop to the basket of a rim-rocking slam dunk that would bring the crowd to its feet. Three other starters, Michael Young, Benny Anders, and Micheaux, also could dunk with ease and Olajuwon, too, had learned to jam shots home from the low post position. A Houston sports writer named Thomas Bonk dubbed the team "Phi Slama Jama" and the name became known nationally. The nickname was a takeoff on the Greek letters used to name college fraternities.

"It just took off nationwide," said Coach Lewis. "They started hearing about Phi Slama Jama. The players took a lot of pride in it."

Although Hakeem was still awkward on offense, he became a force on defense and led the nation in blocked shots. He averaged 13 points and 11 rebounds per game and helped

Houston reach the NCAA Final Four for the second consecutive year.

The semifinal matchup was the game everyone had been waiting for as it pitted the number-one-ranked Cougars against the number-two-ranked University of Louisville. Hakeem responded to the challenge by playing the best game of his career. He had 21 points, 22 rebounds, and 8 blocked shots in leading Houston to a 94-81 victory.

The Cougars were heavily favored to beat North Carolina State in the championship game, and Hakeem had an incredible game with 20 points, 18 rebounds, and 11 blocked shots. But the Wolf-pack scored a stunning upset, winning 54-52 on a last-second follow-up shot by Lorenzo Charles of a desperation heave from near mid-court.

Incredibly, the winning shot had come from right under the basket while Hakeem stood motionless off to the side. As the ball went through the net and the North Carolina State players began a wild celebration, Hakeem fell to the floor crying inconsolably. He was named Most Valuable Player of the tournament, a rarity for someone from a losing team, but the loss haunted him for years.

"It's still the worst day I ever had," Hakeem would say years later. "We were the better team and were supposed to win. The following day when you wake up, it's 'Wow, we lost that game.' You're trying not to think about it, but every time you think about it, it's so depressing."

A shocking defeat such as the one suffered by the Cougars can sometimes destroy a team. On top of that, the team lost Drexler, who decided to pass up his senior year and turn pro, and Micheaux, who graduated. But once again the

Cougars were among the best teams in the nation.

Led by Hakeem, who averaged 16 points per game and led the nation in rebounding (13.5) and field goal percentage (67.5), Houston advanced to the Final Four for the third consecutive year. They squeaked by a surprisingly tough Virginia Commonwealth team in the semifinals, winning in overtime, 49-47. That set up a meeting college basketball fans across the nation were waiting for, a clash of titans between Hakeem and Georgetown's Patrick Ewing.

Although Hakeem scored 15 points and grabbed 9 rebounds, the Cougars were no match for the Hoyas as Georgetown prevailed, 84-75, and Ewing won tournament MVP honors. Hakeem managed only 9 shots in the game and criticized his team for playing selfishly. It was more a case, though, of Georgetown's defense, especially Ewing, stopping the Cougars from getting inside for easier shots.

The Cougars had now failed three years in a row at winning a national championship and Hakeem decided it was time to move on. He passed up his senior year of eligibility and entered the NBA draft. The Rockets had earned the first pick in the draft by winning a coin flip with the Portland Trail Blazers. The Rockets used the pick to select Hakeem. They already had a center in three-time collegiate player of the year Ralph Sampson, but they were ready to begin one of the more fascinating experiments in NBA history. The era of "The Twin Towers" was about to begin.

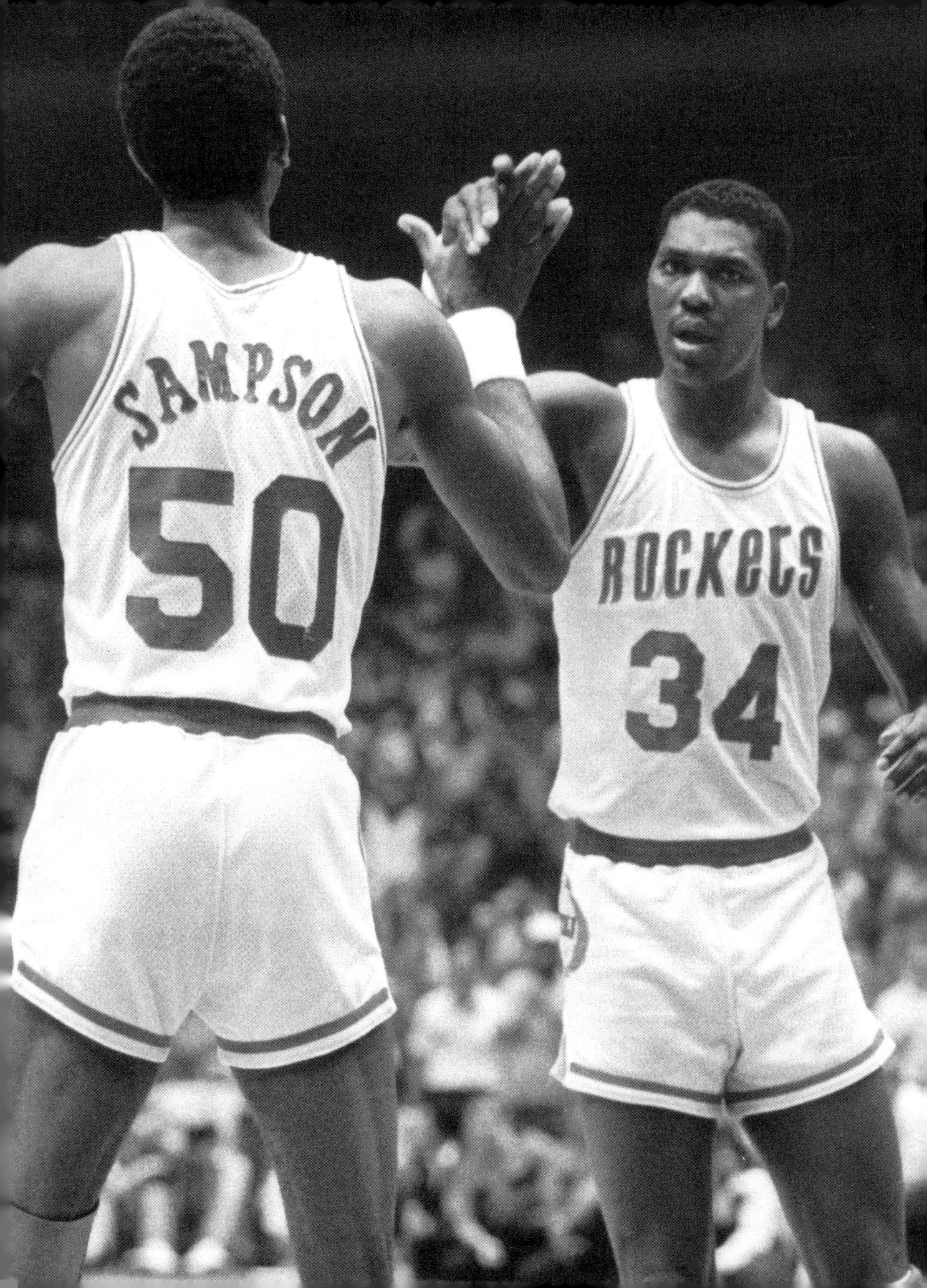
SAMPSON
50
ROCKETS
34

4

THE TWIN TOWERS

The Rockets were in sad shape when Hakeem joined them for the 1984-85 season. Even though Sampson was voted the NBA's Rookie of the Year the previous season, the team won only 29 games.

Coach Bill Fitch decided it was time to try something different. By drafting Hakeem, the Rockets now had two of the quickest big men in the league. Why not put them on the court at the same time?

Although Sampson stood 7'4", he was reed thin and couldn't take the pounding under the boards. Sampson was a graceful athlete and a good shooter for a man his height, so Coach Fitch decided he could better serve the club as a forward. Hakeem would take over the center position.

Some people wondered how Sampson would adjust to the change. After all, he was the star

When the twin towers of Ralph Sampson (7'4") and Hakeem Olajuwon (6'11") exchanged high fives, their hands met in nose-bleed territory.

Olajuwon sometimes let his temper get the best of him. Referee Jess Kersey tries to break up the fight between Hakeem and Mitch Kupchak of the Los Angeles Lakers during the 1986 playoffs.

of the team before Hakeem arrived. But Sampson took the switch very well. "I enjoy it. I definitely enjoy it," said Sampson. "With Hakeem inside, there's less pressure for me to rebound or block shots." It also gave Ralph a better chance to score. Opposing clubs could no longer double or triple-team him. If they did, Hakeem would be able to score himself.

It didn't take Coach Fitch long to realize that he had someone special in Hakeem. Hakeem had a work ethic that Fitch hadn't seen in a long time. He worked constantly at improving his game.

Fitch's bold Twin Towers plan showed early promise. Hakeem established himself as one of the league's best pivot men. He was a unique talent, able to run the court with the speed of a guard and hit the boards with the league's best rebounders.

It seemed certain that he would replace Kareem Abdul-Jabbar of the Los Angeles Lakers as the league's next dominating center.

Sometimes, though, he had trouble understanding what Fitch was talking about. Fitch liked to use American idioms in communicating with his players and Hakeem had trouble understanding what he meant. One day in practice Fitch was correcting an error on the court and said, "There are a lot of guys in Boot Hill who made the same mistake." After the workout, Hakeem asked a teammate, "What is this place Boot Hill?"

On another occasion Fitch noticed something positive in practice and said, "Every now and then a tree grows in Brooklyn." After practice Hakeem inquired of a teammate, "Please tell me, what is this Brooklyn stuff?"

Despite his problems at grasping American expressions, Hakeem had a brilliant rookie season, averaging 20.6 points per game on 53.8 percent shooting from the floor and grabbing 11.9 rebounds per game. Sampson also had a solid season, averaging 22.1 points and 10.9 rebounds per game. The Twin Towers were the first twosome in the NBA to average more than 20 points and 10 rebounds per game since Wilt Chamberlain and Elgin Baylor of the Los Angeles Lakers did it in 1970.

More importantly, however, Hakeem turned the formerly soft Rockets into a defensive force with his shot-blocking and intimidating presence underneath the basket. Rival players found it very difficult to score over the outstretched arms of Hakeem and Sampson. "It was like shooting a basketball into a forest," said Bernard King, a high-scoring forward for the Knicks. "You know you've got a good chance of hitting a branch."

Hakeem finished second to Jordan in the "Rookie of the Year" voting and the Rockets finished second in the NBA's Midwest Division, improving their record of the previous season by 19 games.

Not all was perfect with Hakeem, however. He had a volatile temper that would often explode on the court. He berated officials and got into fights with players from other teams. It would result in technical fouls being called against the Rockets and sometimes cost them the services of their big star.

He also found professional basketball much harder than college basketball. "You have to work for every point you get," said Hakeem. "In college you can get lazy and get away with it. Here, the competition will take advantage."

Coach Fitch was pleased with the team's effort but cautioned that Ralph and Hakeem were still learning the game and not to expect too much from the Rockets too soon.

It turned out the Rockets weren't as far away as Coach Fitch thought. In the 1985-86 season, the Rockets emerged as a power in the Western Conference. Hakeem improved his scoring average to 23.5 on 52.6 percent shooting and continued to rank among the league's leaders in rebounds and blocked shots. He made second team All-NBA, losing out to Abdul-Jabbar by only one vote.

Sampson's statistics also were good and the Rockets went into the playoffs with great confidence. They met the Sacramento Kings in a best-of-five series in the first round and Hakeem set the tone with 29 points in the first game as Houston won, 107-87. The Rockets also won the next two games to sweep the series. Their next opponent was the Denver Nuggets and the Rockets knew they would be tougher.

In a best-of-seven series, Houston won, 4-2, but two of the games went into overtime. In Game 5, with the series tied at two games apiece,

Hakeem scored 36 points to lead Houston to a 131-103 blowout. Game 6 was more exciting. The two teams played two overtimes before Houston finally won, 126-122. Hakeem led the Rockets with 28 points.

Houston's opponent in the Western Conference finals was the Los Angeles Lakers. It meant Hakeem would be playing against the legendary

Bill Walton of the Boston Celtics fouls Olajuwon as Hakeem battles for a rebound with new "twin tower" partner Jim Petersen. Mitch Wiggins tries not to get hurt during the 1986 playoff action.

Kareem Abdul-Jabbar. Kareem was 39 years old, but he still had plenty of skills. He was named MVP of the finals the previous season.

The much publicized matchup of the league's two premier big men wasn't much of a contest. Hakeem completely dominated Kareem and the Rockets eliminated the defending league champions in five games. Hakeem was unstoppable, averaging 30 points, 12 rebounds, and 4 blocked shots.

Hakeem's performance caused the Lakers' all-star guard Earvin "Magic" Johnson to marvel, "In terms of raw athletic ability, Hakeem is the best I've ever seen."

The Rockets met the Boston Celtics in the championship series and Hakeem knew his team would be in for a rough battle. The Celtics had won the Eastern Division three straight years and four of the last six. They had a lot of depth and their front line of Larry Bird, Kevin McHale, and Robert Parish was the best in the league.

Hakeem played superbly in the series and dominated the two centers who tried to contain him, Parish and Bill Walton. But the Celtics had a deeper bench and more overall balance. Led by Bird, the league's MVP, the Celtics beat the Rockets in six games to win the NBA title.

Houston, though, had served notice that it was the team to beat in the West and other teams began copying the Rockets' Twin Towers approach.

Hakeem and his teammates thought that the Rockets would certainly battle for the league title again in 1986-87. But, even though Hakeem averaged 23.9 points per game that season, the club's lack of consistent play from the back court caused the team to be eliminated in the second round of the playoffs.

The team was falling apart. Guards Mitch Wiggins and Lewis Lloyd were suspended for breaking the league's drug rules and Ralph Sampson began to suffer a series of injuries that would eventually bring a premature end to his career. Still, Hakeem refused to give in. He did his best to try and take the team to the NBA finals anyway. He had a standout season in 1986-87, finishing his third year as a pro with a scoring average of 23.4 points per game — twelfth best average in the league. He also finished eighth in the league in rebounds and third in blocked shots. He led the Rockets in 13 categories and was named first team all-NBA for his first time.

Thanks to Hakeem's play, the Rockets made the playoffs and were matched against Portland in the first round. Hakeem's old buddy from college, Clyde Drexler, was the star of the Trail Blazers, but Portland could not stop Hakeem. The Rockets won the series, three games to one.

They advanced to meet the Seattle SuperSonics and Hakeem continued his scoring blitz, including a high of 49 points in Game 6. But the SuperSonics were deeper than the Rockets and won the series, four games to two.

When the Rockets started slowly in the 1987–88 season, the Twin Towers experiment ended. Sampson was traded to the Detroit Pistons in December of 1987. By the end of the season, Coach Fitch was gone too, and the Rockets were preparing to head in another direction.

5

THE SEARCH

The Rockets' continued mediocrity was wearing on Olajuwon. During the 1987-88 campaign, he finished among the league's top 10 in scoring, rebounding, blocked shots, and steals, but when the team was eliminated by Dallas in the first round of the playoffs he blew up at his teammates. Hakeem accused them of not caring. He also criticized the Rockets' management for bringing in players who were not wanted elsewhere.

Don Chaney, a former star at both the University of Houston and with the Rockets, was named as Fitch's successor to start the 1988-89 campaign and Hakeem had another dominating year. He became the first player in league history to collect more than 200 steals (213) and blocks (282) in a season and also led the league in rebounding. The Rockets posted a 45-37 record, which was good enough to finish second

Cleveland Cavalier forward Larry Nance stands like a statue as Hakeem Olajuwon shows off his mobility, bolting around him for an easy hoop.

in their division, but once again they fell in the first round of the playoffs.

It was more of the same the following season. Hakeem led the league in rebounding and blocked shots in 1989-90, but the Rockets struggled to play .500 ball and were eliminated by the Lakers in the first round of the playoffs.

Hakeem's career almost came to a sudden end on January 3, 1991. The Rockets were playing the Chicago Bulls and Hakeem was accidentally hit in the face by an elbow from the Bulls' center Bill Cartwright. The bone around Hakeem's right eye was fractured and he was out of action for 25 games.

His injury seemed to serve as a wake-up call for the team. Instead of giving up because their star center was hurt, the Rockets rallied behind guard Vernon Maxwell, forward Otis Thorpe, and journeyman center Larry Smith, who replaced Hakeem in the middle. They won 15 of the games Hakeem missed and when he did return he played six games as Smith's backup so as not to disrupt the team's chemistry.

The Rockets rattled off 13 victories in a row and appeared to be the team to beat for the NBA title. But when they hit the playoffs they fell flat again. The Lakers beat them, three games to none, in the first round of the playoffs.

During his years in the NBA, Hakeem had developed an image as a malcontent because of

After Olajuwon took an elbow to the face from Bill Cartwright of the Chicago Bulls, Adrian Caldwell helped carry his teammate off on a stretcher.

his constant sniping at teammates and his contract arguments with the Rockets' front office. But now he began a feud with Rockets' owner, Charlie Thomas.

Hakeem was in the middle of a five-year, $18.3-million contract and asked Thomas to renegotiate it, even though he had promised he would not seek a new deal. The Rockets had been happy to oblige Hakeem in the past by renegotiating contracts, but not this time. Thomas stood firm.

Early in the 1991-92 season, Hakeem received a scare. His heart started beating irregularly and he had to have medical treatment to correct it. He missed seven games between November 23 and December 6.

Then in March of 1992, Hakeem refused to suit up for a game. He said he had a pulled hamstring. The Rockets did not believe him. They thought he was faking the injury in order to put himself in a better bargaining position. General Manager Steve Patterson suspended Hakeem for three games.

Even when Hakeem returned to the lineup the team did not play well. They lost four of their final five games and missed the playoffs for the first time since 1983-84, the season before Hakeem joined the team. Moreover, Thomas was trying to sell the team and that infuriated Hakeem even more. He demanded to be traded.

The Rockets actually tried to trade him. They talked to the Miami Heat and the Los Angeles Clippers but no deal could be worked out. Even during this period of discontent with Houston management, Hakeem continued to follow a strict work ethic. During the off season he took 500 shots a day to improve his 15-foot jumper.

Hakeem may not have been aware of it at the time, but two changes were taking place in his life that would enable him to achieve his greatest heights both as a person and a professional athlete. The first had to do with religion; the second was the naming of former Rockets' star Rudy Tomjanovich as coach of the team.

Hakeem had known for years that something was missing from his spiritual life. As a youngster growing up in Nigeria he had been raised as a Muslim. Nearly half of all Nigerians belong to the religion of Islam. Muslims do not drink alcohol or eat pork or gamble. Five times a day they kneel to pray while facing in the direction of their holy city, Mecca, which is located in the Middle Eastern nation of Saudi Arabia.

Hakeem had left his religion behind in Nigeria when he left for the University of Houston. But in 1990, Hakeem felt the urge to return to the religion of his roots. He found a mosque in Houston and began studying the Koran.

By 1992, the spirituality of his religion was slowly changing Hakeem. He no longer argued with referees. He was polite to everyone. The man who once punched out teammate Derek Chievous in the locker room now spoke of the need for grace and harmony among neighbors.

"It's not a matter of maturity; it's the knowledge of *din*," said Olajuwon. "The Book of the Prophet says that when Allah blesses a person, He gives him the knowledge of *din*. Some think of *din* as religion, but it's more than that. It's a way of life, a state. You know man's origin and purpose. You have vision. You have a goal. You see things differently and act differently. You look at the overall picture. *Din* becomes a way of life."

On road trips Hakeem began taking a prayer rug and a special compass that pointed him in the direction of Mecca. He began fasting on holy days, learned to recite the Koran, and regularly scheduled afternoon prayer sessions.

"Islam has helped put everything in perspective," he said. "In this business, with so much material wealth and fame, Islam allows you to see that material things are nothing but conveniences of life. You have money, what do you do? Have a better car? More cars? Bigger house? But that which is God is more enduring and everlasting."

While his religion brought him peace of mind it ended up costing him his relationship with his girl friend, Lita Spencer. He had met Lita when he was at the University of Houston. They had moved in together in 1986 and had a daughter, Abisola, in 1988. But Lita did not wish to convert to Islam. The two broke up.

Hakeem's religion helped make him a better basketball player by giving him more confidence in himself. His teammates could see it.

"I've always believed off-court life affects on-court success — and Hakeem's game has new peace because of the peace he's found away from the game," said Rockets' point guard Kenny Smith.

The arrival of Tomjanovich, who succeeded Chaney as coach, helped Hakeem become a better all-around player. Rudy T, as he was affectionately called by players and fans alike, had been a five-time All-Star forward for the Rockets in the 1970s and was beloved in Houston.

He had spent his entire 11-year playing career with the Rockets and had his jersey retired in January of 1982. Moreover, he had spent his entire career in professional basketball with the Rockets, a span of 22 years. For the past nine years he had served as an assistant coach.

On February 18, 1992, Rudy T was named to succeed Chaney as head coach. The team responded by winning 11 of its first 15 games — the best start by any coach in franchise history. The team finished the season 16-14 under Tomjanovich, but the way he treated his players gave reason to believe there would be great times ahead for the Rockets.

One of the first things Tomjanovich did when he took over the Rockets was to pay a visit on team owner Charlie Thomas and general manager Steve Patterson. Rudy wanted to keep Hakeem on the team and he wanted to make his case with upper management.

A doctor's examination had confirmed that Hakeem's leg had been hurt as he had claimed. He had not been lying to management. Tomjanovich stated his case well. Before the beginning of the 1992-93 season, Hakeem and Thomas ended their dispute. Thomas agreed to a $25.4-million extension of Hakeem's contract through 1999.

On the court, Tomjanovich designed a new system that had Hakeem as the central figure. The guards would pass the ball inside to Hakeem and he would decide whether to go to the basket or pass the ball back outside. Aided by his now consistent jump shot, he responded by posting career bests in scoring (26.1 points per game) and, more important, assists (291). His new willingness to give up the ball boosted the confidence of his teammates, who supported him better than they ever had before.

The Rockets prospered under the new system. They won a club record 55 games and finished first in the Midwest Division for the first time since 1986. In the playoffs, the Rockets squeezed past the Los Angeles Clippers in the opening round but then lost to the Seattle SuperSonics in a tough seven-game series.

Hakeem excelled on defense as well as offense. He led the league in blocked shots for the third time (342) and was fourth in rebounding (13.0). In addition, his 150 steals were better than all other centers. He also became only the second player in NBA history to have more than 250 assists and 300 blocks in the same year and the third player to accumulate 2,000 points, 1,000 rebounds, and 300 blocks in the same year.

He was named the NBA's Defensive Player of the Year and finished second in the MVP voting. Clearly, he had established himself as the premier center in the league. But one thing was missing — a championship.

"Hakeem has as much influence on the game of basketball as any player in the league," said Seattle coach George Karl. "If he never wins a title, I think it hurts him. I don't think there's any question that the great ones, the ones who are thought of with reverence, have to win a title."

But with Rudy T at the helm and Hakeem playing his best basketball, it seemed only a matter of time before the Rockets earned that championship pennant.

6

THE PINNACLE

If that championship was to come, though, Charlie Thomas was not going to be part of it. The cost of owning a professional sports team had become too expensive and so, on July 30, 1993, Thomas sold the Rockets to Leslie L. Alexander. Three days after Alexander took over the team the Rockets bolstered their team by making a trade with the Portland Trail Blazers to acquire the versatile Mario Elie. Earlier, the Rockets had drafted guard Sam Cassell out of Florida State. Cassell had been a second-team all-Atlantic Coast Conference selection and was a good shooter and excellent defensive player.

With Hakeem leading the way, the Rockets went undefeated in November, winning 14 games to take an early lead in the standings. Hakeem averaged 25.4 points, 13.5 rebounds, 4.1 blocks, and 3.3 assists to earn Player of the Month honors.

Hakeem was not the only one playing well. Vernon Maxwell, Otis Thorpe, and Robert Horry all

Hakeem Olajuwon rejects a shot from Utah Jazz guard John Stockton during playoff action in 1994.

were averaging in double figures. The Rockets won their first game in December to tie the record set by the 1948-49 Washington Capitals for the best start in NBA history.

The Atlanta Hawks beat the Rockets to stop their streak, but by December 23, 1993, the Rockets were 22-2. On January 21st, Hakeem turned 31 years old. The wear and tear of jumping, jostling for position, and running the court often ends centers' careers by the time they hit 30, but Olajuwon was getting better with age. He averaged nearly 30 points per game in January and more than 25 points in February. He was selected to start at center for the Western Conference in the All-Star game for the fifth time in his career.

Hakeem had become so well-known nationally he was even used as the inspiration for a movie called *The Air Up There*, which was released in 1994. The screenplay was written by Max Apple, a Houston-based author, and revolved around a character named Jimmy Dolan, an ambitious assistant basketball coach who goes off to Africa to try and recruit a tall black youth.

The Air Up There *is a movie loosely based on Hakeem Olajuwon's life story. In this scene, Kevin Bacon (right) plays an assistant college basketball coach trying to recruit a tall tribal warrior with excellent basketball skills played by Charles Gitonga Maina (left).*

March was an even better month for the Rockets. They went 9-1 at home and enjoyed their second-best March in franchise history. They held onto first place in the Midwest Division for the fourth month in a row.

In April, the Rockets clinched their second straight Midwest division title by defeating the

Trail Blazers, 119-110. The victory was their 58th of the season, a club record. Hakeem finished the season averaging a career best 27.3 points per game. He also averaged 11.9 rebounds and once again showed his ability to pass the ball by picking up 287 assists. It was no surprise when he was named the league's Most Valuable Player.

The Rockets were confident that this would be the season they claimed the NBA title. But just as the players began thinking about the playoffs, a rash of injuries hit the team. Although no one likes to tinker with team chemistry late in the year, the Rockets were forced to add two new players: forward Earl Cureton and guard Larry Robinson.

Just before the start of the best-of-five first round playoff series against Portland, the injured Rockets' players got healthy again. Houston won the first two games, but Portland came back to win Game 3 before the Rockets put them away in Game 4.

The second round was a best-of-seven series and the Rockets faced the Phoenix Suns, whose star, Charles Barkley, had beaten out Hakeem for the league's MVP award in 1992-93. Houston had the home court advantage for the series and built an 18-point lead in Game 1. But the Rockets collapsed late in the game and lost, 91-87, before a stunned crowd at The Summit. The same thing happened in Game 2 and suddenly the Rockets found themselves trailing, 2-0, with the series now switching to Phoenix. Houston fans wondered if this would be another one of those underachieving Rockets' teams.

Hakeem would not let his team quit, however. The Rockets bounced back to win Games 3 and 4 and the America West Arena, sending the series back to Houston. The Rockets won game 5 and needed just one more victory to advance to the Western Conference championship. But the Rockets lost game 6 in Phoenix, setting up the showdown game in Houston.

Hakeem was simply awesome in Game 7. The Suns had no one who could contain him. He finished with 37 points, 17 rebounds, and 3 blocked shots in leading the Rockets to a 104-94 victory.

Houston's opponent in the Western Conference finals was the Utah Jazz and they were no match for the inspired Rockets. Houston won the best-of-seven series in five games. After eight years the Rockets were finally returning to the NBA championship round.

Coach Tomjanovich was delighted that the Rockets' opponent was New York. It would mean more media would be covering the game and it would get his players, especially Hakeem, more publicity. Rudy T wanted basketball fans across the country to know how great Hakeem was. "I really feel great that the country can see what kind of person he is," said Tomjanovich.

Hakeem was up to the challenge of Ewing in the first game. He outscored the Knicks' star, 28-23, and the Rockets won, 85-78.

In Game 2 the Knicks pushed and grabbed Hakeem in an effort to keep him off the boards. The strategy worked. Although Hakeem scored 25 points, he managed only 7 rebounds and the Knicks won, 91-83.

The Rockets came back to win Game 3, then New York rebounded to take games 4 and 5. The series shifted back to Houston and the Rockets were on the brink of being eliminated.

In Game 6, the Rockets built a 10-point lead only to see the Knicks pull within two points with only seconds remaining. New York had the ball for the last shot and John Starks's attempt was partially blocked by Hakeem as the Rockets hung on to win, 86-84, and even the series. If the Rockets could win Game 7 they would be NBA champions.

In the final game, four Rockets scored in double figures and they edged the Knicks, 90-84, to bring Houston its first championship in any sport.

For Hakeem, the excitement was not so much in winning the championship but experiencing the ordeal in getting there. "The joy of it is the experience of coming through it," said Hakeem. "Looking back at the tough series with Portland; being down 0-2 to Phoenix and coming back to win; beating Utah; losing home-court advantage to New York then going out there and winning the first game. That's what I enjoy now when I look back. You have to enjoy the journey, not just the destination."

After the Rockets won the 1994 championship, they were invited to the White House. Coach Rudy Tomjon-avich is to the right of President Bill Clinton and Hakeem Olajuwon is to his left. To Hakeem's left are Scott Brooks, Kenny Smith, Sam Cassell, and Mario Elie.

7

CHAMPS AGAIN

Winning an NBA title often can lead to many endorsements for the players on the championship team. Especially for someone as regal in appearance and demeanor as Hakeem. But it did not turn out that way for the Rockets. It was clear that most of the basketball world thought the title was a fluke. And despite projecting an image of class and reliability, Hakeem was not being besieged with offers from advertisers.

"Madison Avenue prefers an American guy," said Marty Blackman, whose firm, Blackman & Raber, matches athletes with advertisers. "Is that a disadvantage? Yes. No question. It's not racial. It's just a fact."

Hakeem also was at a disadvantage because his team played in Houston and not New York or Chicago. In addition, he was not a flashy type

Hakeem Olajuwon and Charles Jones fight for rebounding position against Dennis Rodman of the San Antonio Spurs during 1995 playoff action.

Shaquille O'Neal of the Magic had good statistics in the 1995 playoff finals against the Rockets. But Olajuwon had even better stats—and Houston defeated Orlando in four straight games to win back-to-back championships.

or a trash talker or a backboard breaker. The lack of sponsors knocking on the door did not bother Hakeem. He had a policy not to be a spokesman for any product he did not believe in or products that he considered harmful.

"How can a poor working mother with three boys buy Nikes or Reeboks that cost $120?" wondered Hakeem. "She can't. So kids steal these shoes from stores and other kids. Sometimes they kill for them."

Hakeem was more concerned in getting the Rockets the respect they deserved on the basketball court. When the preseason predictions came out, hardly anyone picked the Rockets to repeat as NBA champions. Hakeem took the slight as a challenge. He would prove everyone wrong.

His teammates felt the same way. "I guess we'll just have to do it all over again," said guard Sam Cassell.

The team started off well, winning nine games in a row early in the campaign. Even after the team went into a brief slump in mid-December, Hakeem wasn't worried.

"The league is very well-balanced now," said Hakeem. "You look around and there are good teams everywhere. It would be very difficult for us to dominate the league in an 82-game season. We'll have to make a commitment to excellence in order to get back to the way we were playing."

Part of the problem was injuries. Six of Hakeem's teammates missed 10 or more games during the season. Vernon Maxwell was suspended for 10 games for going into the stands and hitting a fan. Even Hakeem missed some time because of injury. Early in the season he tripped and fell over a TV cameraman stationed near the out-of-bounds line. He cut his hand and hurt his wrist and missed one game.

But the Rockets also lacked the intensity they had shown the previous year. As mid-season approached, the team was still floundering. Coach Tomjanovich knew something had to be done to inject life into the team. So he engineered a trade with the Portland Trail Blazers to obtain veteran All-Star guard Clyde Drexler, Hakeem's former college teammate. Although one of the top players in the league, Clyde had never been part of an NBA championship team.

In exchange, Tomjanovich was forced to give up forward Otis Thorpe, a rugged rebounder who had been a key part of the championship team the previous season.

Not all the players welcomed the trade.

"I didn't like it at first," said Robert Horry. "Otis was an important part of our team winning that first championship. We were trading away rebounding, which we badly needed, for a position we were deep at."

Tomjanovich thought Drexler would bring some much needed energy to the team. And he was right. Drexler knew this might be his last chance to play on a winner. He was determined to do whatever it took to get the Rockets on track toward another NBA crown.

"He brought a new dimension to the team," said Hakeem of his friend. "He brought experience, an ability to steal the ball. He created a lot of problems for the opponent by grabbing a rebound off the defensive boards and taking it coast-to-coast."

The team improved somewhat after Drexler's arrival, but in March the club received a jolt when it was learned that Hakeem was suffering from anemia, which means his blood lacked iron. He had hypothyroidism, which means his thyroid gland was working too slowly.

When the Rockets' fans learned what had caused this weakened condition they were stunned. Hakeem had been going without food from daybreak to sundown during the holy month of Ramadan and getting weaker every day. He had placed his religious obligations as a Muslim before his duty to the team.

Rockets' boosters begged him to stop. But he would not. He continued fasting until he had starved himself into an iron deficiency and a thyroid condition. Soon he was so weak that he had to be benched for two weeks.

To the astonishment of all, Hakeem came back near the end of the season and played as well as he had in the previous season when he was the league's MVP. He scored an average of 27.8 points per game, grabbed 10.8 rebounds, and had 3.76 blocked shots. He had five more steals than he had in the previous year, even though he played eight fewer games.

The Rockets stumbled home with a 47-25 record and were seeded sixth in the conference playoffs. No team seeded as low as sixth had ever won the league title before. "This is definitely not where we want to be," Hakeem said as the Rockets prepared to face the Jazz, in Utah, in the first round of the playoffs. "But these are the cards we have been dealt. It takes all the pressure off us in this series. Nobody expects us to win."

One game into the postseason playoffs, the Rockets were hit with another crisis. Vernon Maxwell, whose minutes had diminished with the acquisition of Drexler, said he could not handle his new role of coming off the bench and took a leave of absence.

It took an outstanding effort by Hakeem for the Rockets to survive the first round. He scored 40 points and then 33 as Houston won the final two games, including the last one on the road, to upset the Jazz.

Now an American citizen, Olajuwon proudly models the jersey he wore during the 1996 Olympics.

The Rockets then met the Phoenix Suns and it looked as if their quest for a second straight championship was over when the Suns took a 3-1 lead in the best-of-seven series. Remarkably, Hakeem rallied his team. The Rockets won the next three games to advance to the championship round.

Houston's opponent in the Western Conference finals was San Antonio, which featured David Robinson, one of the league's most dominating centers. Robinson won that year's MVP award, but he was no match for Hakeem, who led the Rockets to a victory in six games.

It became clear to everyone early on that the question wasn't who was the better center, but where did Hakeem stand among the best centers of all time.

"No question about it, he's a phenomenal player," said Dave Cowens, a former San Antonio assistant coach and NBA All-Star center. "If you look at the way he's built, he's a big guy but his center of gravity is remarkable. He doesn't really have long legs or a long torso. It's great for balance. Plus he's got the soccer background, and he's got a great amount of concentration. He doesn't get distracted at all."

Hakeem had disposed of Robinson. Now he faced another stern test. The Orlando Magic and their 7'1", 320-pound center Shaquille O'Neal had won the Eastern Conference title for the first time. O'Neal had averaged 25 points and 12 rebounds a game with a power game that was at times mind-boggling.

But Hakeem had the better all-around game, plus the experience of having played in a championship round. It made for an interesting comparison.

"Whoever does a better job from the post of reading the defense is going to win the series," said veteran coach Pete Newell, who had taught both O'Neal and Hakeem the importance of good footwork.

O'Neal performed very well in his first championship series. But Hakeem was, well, a Dream. He played superbly, whether it was scoring with his deadly turnaround jumper, grabbing an important rebound, or hitting the open man with a pinpoint pass. The Rockets swept the young Magic in four games to win the championship for the second straight season. Hakeem joined Chicago's Michael Jordan as the only players ever to win back-to-back MVP awards in the playoffs.

"Hakeem is the best basketball player," Rockets' guard Kenny Smith said. "Michael Jordan is a close second right now. But in terms of right this second, Hakeem is the best basketball player. He's on a different level. Jordan's the only one I've seen take it to that level. Right now Hakeem is there. It makes the game easier for everybody."

By winning two straight championships, the Rockets joined Boston, Los Angeles/Minneapolis, Chicago, and Detroit as the only teams to accomplish that feat.

The victory also brought Hakeem some long overdue recognition. He appeared on NBC's "Today Show" and made a second appearance on the "David Letterman Show." He signed contracts to represent Uncle Ben's Rice, M&M Mars bars, and Minolta cameras.

In 1996, the Rockets again suffered numerous injuries to key players, including Olajuwon. They were mostly healthy when playoff time rolled around, but their subpar record meant they didn't have home-court advantage in any of their series.

Houston defeated a tough Los Angeles Lakers team that featured Magic Johnson's last hurrah in the first round, but then fell in the second round to the Seattle Super Sonics. Many Rockets were frustrated by the bruising battles, but Olajuwon was philosophical. "Two championships," he said. "I will be forever grateful."

He was thrilled though when he finally received permission from officials at the International Basketball Federation to play for the United States in the 1996 Olympic Summer Games in Atlanta, Georgia. Dream Team III won the gold medal everyone predicted they would.

It seems hard to believe, but Hakeem may be getting better as a player with each year that passes. "One of the biggest pet peeves with some players is that they don't work at their game," said Rockets' owner Leslie Alexander. "Some guys are the same player five years later. But Hakeem never stops working. He's more focused than ever. Sometimes when you watch him on the court, you'll catch him smiling. He just seems so happy."

STATISTICS

COLLEGE STATISTICS
University of Houston

YEAR	G	PTS	PPG	REB	RPG	B	BPG
1982-83	29	240	8.3	179	6.2	72	2.5
1982-83	34	472	13.9	388	11.4	175	5.1
1983-84	37	620	16.8	500	13.5	207	5.6
Totals	90	1,332	13.3	1,067	10.7	454	4.5

PRO STATISTICS
Houston Rockets

YEAR	G	PTS	PPG	REB	RPG	B	BPG
1984-85	82	1692	20.6	974	11.9	220	2.7
1985-86	68	1597	23.5	781	11.5	231	3.4
1986-87	75	1755	23.4	858	11.4	**254**	3.4
1987-88	79	1805	22.8	959	12.1	214	2.7
1988-89	82	2034	24.8	**1105**	**13.5**	282	3.4
1989-90	82	1995	24.3	**1149**	**14.0**	**376**	4.6
1990-91	56	1187	21.2	770	13.8	221	3.9
1991-92	70	1510	21.6	845	12.1	304	4.3
1992-93	82	2140	26.1	1068	13.0	**342**	4.2
1993-94	80	2184	27.3	955	11.9	297	3.7
1994-95	72	2005	27.8	775	10.8	242	3.4
1995-96	72	1942	27.0	784	10.9	207	2.9
Totals	900	21,846	24.3	11,023	12.2	3,190	3.5

		bold indicates league-leading statistics
G	games
PTS	points
PPG	points per game
REB	rebounds
RPG	rebounds per game
B	blocks
BPG	blocks per game

HAKEEM OLAJUWON
A CHRONOLOGY

1963   Born on January 21 in Lagos, Nigeria.

1980   Introduced to basketball by Oscar Johnson, coach of the Nigerian national team; Christopher Pond paves the way for Hakeem to go to college in the United States.

1982   With Hakeem as a sub, University of Houston reaches Final Four of NCAA Tournament.

1983   Hakeem becomes starting center and Houston is ranked number one in the nation for most of the season; Cougars are upset in championship game by North Carolina State.

1984   Leads Houston to NCAA championship game for second straight year.

1985   Houston Rockets choose Olajuwon with their number one pick in the draft; finishes second in Rookie of the Year voting to Michael Jordan.

1986   Averages 23.5 points per game and makes second team all-NBA; leads Rockets into championship finals where they lose to Boston Celtics.

1987   Named to first team all-NBA for first time.

1989   Becomes first player in NBA history to lead league in steals (213) and blocked shots (282) in same season.

1990   Leads league in rebounds and blocked shots.

1993   Leads team to club record 55 victories and Western Conference title after new coach Rudy Tomjanovich designs an offense centered around Hakeem; named NBA's Defensive Player of Year and finishes second in MVP voting.

1994   Named MVP of league after leading Rockets to club record 58 victories and Midwest Division title; sparks Rockets to first NBA championship; named MVP of playoffs.

1995   Powers Rockets to surprising second NBA championship as they beat Orlando Magic in the finals; named MVP of playoffs for second year in row.

1996   Earns Olympic gold medal as member of U.S. Dream Team III.

SUGGESTIONS FOR FURTHER READING

Barry Bloom, "Hakeem Olajuwon: His Decade in the NBA Has Been an Ever-Ascending Journey." *Sport*, January 1995.

Barry Bloom, "Dream Fulfilled: Two Straight Titles Have Rocketed Hakeem Olajuwon Into Another Dimension." *Sport*, November 1995.

Brad Darrach, "A Different Kind of Superstar." *Life*, December 1995.

Jack McCallum, "A Dream Come True." *Sports Illustrated*, April 22, 1993.

Mark Starr, "Good Enough to Dream; After Two NBA Titles, Hakeem Olajuwon is Running out of Worlds to Conquer." *Newsweek*, November 6, 1995.

ABOUT THE AUTHOR

Fred McMane has been in sports journalism for more than 30 years. He worked for United Press International from 1964-93, serving as a sports writer and editor, including sports editor (1988-93). He is the author of seven books on sports and numerous magazine articles. He is married and the father of three daughters and lives in Millburn, New Jersey.

PICTURE CREDITS: UPI/Corbis-Bettmann: 2, 14, 20; AP/Wide World Photos: 8, 12, 23, 24, 26, 40, 52, 54, 58; Courtesy University of Texas at San Antonio: 17; UPI/Bettmann: 30, 32, 35, 38; Reuters-Bettmann, 46; Official White House Photo, 51.

INDEX